LIBRARY OF
AWESOME ANIMALS

PUFFER FISH

By Rachel Rose

BEARPORT
PUBLISHING

Minneapolis, Minnesota

Credits

Cover and title page, © Nuture/iStock, © Nicoproductions/iStock, © meltonmedia/iStock; 3, © Audrey/Adobe Stock; 4–5, © engabito/iStock; 6–7, © JerryLudwig/iStock; 9, © Jerry Widjojo/Shutterstock; 10–11, © Hannalvanova/Adobe Stock; 13, © Matt9122/Shutterstock, © SergeUWPhoto/Shutterstock; 14, © vkilikov/Shutterstock; 15, © Ludovicanigro/Shutterstock; 16, © unknown author/Wikimedia Commons; 17, © mirecca/Adobe Stock; 18–19, © cbimages/Alamy; 20–21, © SaltedLife/Shutterstock; 22, © Jamie Depledge/Shutterstock, © Tiia Monto/Wikimedia Commons; 23, © Alex Churilov/Adobe Stock.

Bearport Publishing Company Product Development Team

President: Jen Jenson; Director of Product Development: Spencer Brinker; Managing Editor: Allison Juda; Associate Editor: Naomi Reich; Associate Editor: Tiana Tran; Senior Designer: Colin O'Dea; Associate Designer: Elena Klinkner; Associate Designer: Kayla Eggert; Product Development Specialist: Anita Stasson

Library of Congress Cataloging-in-Publication Data

Names: Rose, Rachel, 1968- author.
Title: Puffer fish / by Rachel Rose.
Description: Minneapolis, Minnesota : Bearport Publishing Company, [2024] |
  Series: Library of awesome animals | Includes bibliographical references
  and index.
Identifiers: LCCN 2023005357 (print) | LCCN 2023005358 (ebook) | ISBN
  9798885099967 (hardcover) | ISBN 9798888221792 (paperback) | ISBN
  9798888223116 (ebook)
Subjects: LCSH: Puffers (Fish)--Juvenile literature.
Classification: LCC QL638.T32 R67 2024 (print) | LCC QL638.T32 (ebook) |
  DDC 597/.64--dc23/eng/20230302
LC record available at https://lccn.loc.gov/2023005357
LC ebook record available at https://lccn.loc.gov/2023005358

For more information, write to Bearport Publishing, 5357 Penn Avenue South, Minneapolis, MN 55419.

Contents

AWESOME
Puffer Fish!

POOF! A puffer fish blows up to twice its normal size to scare off a **predator**. With balloon-shaped bodies and spiney skin, puffer fish are awesome!

PUFFER FISH ARE ALSO CALLED BLOWFISH, SWELLFISH, OR PUFFERS.

Warm at Home

There are many different kinds of puffer fish living in warm waters around the world. Most are found in oceans near colorful **coral reefs**. Puffer fish have skin with lots of patterns or colors to help them blend in with their bright homes. Most of the time they look a lot like other fish. But every once in a while, they puff up like balloons.

SOME PUFFER FISH LIVE IN RIVERS AND LAKES. THEIR SKIN IS USUALLY DULL TO MATCH THESE HABITATS.

Underwater Balloons

When in danger, puffers can swell to more than twice their normal size. They puff up by filling their very stretchy stomachs with large amounts of water or air. Once inflated, most puffer fish have spines that stick out from their skin. Not only do they look too big to eat, but also their spikes make them look too prickly for hungry predators!

IT'S DIFFICULT FOR PUFFERS TO SWIM WHEN INFLATED. THEY OFTEN FLOAT AROUND UNTIL THEY RETURN TO NORMAL.

Quick Getaway

Puffer fish have more than one way of staying safe. If puffers keep close watch, they may not need to puff up. That's because they have excellent eyesight! If they spot predators, the fish swim away in a sudden burst of speed. They use their tail fins to quickly push themselves along.

PUFFER FISH CAN MOVE EACH EYE SEPARATELY. THIS HELPS THEM SPOT DANGER FASTER.

Puffer Poison

If a predator does eat a puffer fish, it may be in for a deadly surprise! Nearly all kinds of puffers are **poisonous**. The poison is in every part of the fish. Just touching the skin of a puffer is dangerous. Most hungry animals that make a snack of a puffer will die. *YIKES!*

PUFFER FISH ARE THE MOST POISONOUS ANIMALS IN THE SEA.

Terrific Teeth

Escaping enemies can make puffers hungry. What do these fish eat? Their diet is made up of **algae** as well as other fish. They also chow down on shellfish, including mussels and clams. Puffers crack through hard shells with four superstrong teeth. *CRUNCH!* Their chompers are joined together in a shape that looks like a beak.

PUFFER FISH TEETH NEVER STOP GROWING. EATING THROUGH HARD SHELLS KEEPS THE TEETH TRIMMED.

Dance Circle

When it's time to have babies, puffer fish choose a **mate**. Some puffer **males** do a special dance, swimming in circles at the bottom of the ocean to attract a partner. If a **female** likes the dance, she will swim to the center of the circle.

THE MALE PUFFER FISH DANCE CREATES CIRCLE PATTERNS IN THE SAND ON THE SEA FLOOR.

Egg Delivery

Other puffers pick a partner closer to shore. Once one of these females has picked her mate, the mate may help push her to shallow water. There, the female lays eggs. Sometimes, the male will rub her belly to help push out the eggs. Then, the male **fertilizes** them.

A FEMALE PUFFER LAYS BETWEEN THREE AND SEVEN EGGS AT A TIME.

Small Fry, Big Puffers

After about a week, the eggs are ready to **hatch**. Puffer babies are called **fry**, and they are tiny. If small fry were to puff up, they wouldn't scare away hungry predators. Luckily, they are born with poison on their skin. This helps keep them safe as they get bigger. After a few months, they can puff up with power!

PUFFER FISH ARE AWESOME!
LET'S LEARN EVEN MORE ABOUT THEM.

Kind of animal: Puffer fish are fish. Like all fish, they are cold-blooded animals that breathe with gills.

More puffer fish: There are more than 120 kinds of puffer fish, including the tiger puffer fish, sharpnose puffer, and red-eyed puffer fish.

Size: Different kinds of puffers are different sizes, but the largest can be up to 3 feet (90 cm) long. That's as long as a baseball bat.

PUFFER FISH AROUND THE WORLD

Arctic Ocean
NORTH AMERICA
EUROPE
ASIA
Pacific Ocean
Atlantic Ocean
AFRICA
Pacific Ocean
SOUTH AMERICA
Indian Ocean
AUSTRALIA
N W E S
Southern Ocean
WHERE PUFFER FISH LIVE
ANTARCTICA

Glossary

algae tiny plantlike living things that grow in water

coral reefs rocklike structures formed from the skeletons of sea animals

female a puffer fish that can lay eggs

fertilizes makes eggs able to grow into baby fish

fry baby fish

habitats places in nature where animals live

hatch to come out of an egg

males puffer fish that cannot lay eggs

mate a partner chosen for having young

poisonous able to kill or cause harm

predator an animal that hunts and eats other animals

23

Index

Read More

Gunasekara, Mignonne. *Fantastic Fish (At the Aquarium).* Minneapolis: Bearport Publishing Company, 2021.

Phillips, Howard. *Beware the Puffer Fish (Poisonous Creatures).* New York: Enslow Publishing, 2023.

Learn More Online

1. Go to **www.factsurfer.com** or scan the QR code below.
2. Enter "**Puffer Fish**" into the search box.
3. Click on the cover of this book to see a list of websites.

About the Author

Rachel Rose writes books for kids and teaches yoga. She lives in California with her favorite animal—her dog, Sandy.